Horsefly Dress

HEATHER CAHOON

Horsefly Dress

POEMS

THE UNIVERSITY OF
ARIZONA PRESS

TUCSON

The University of Arizona Press
www.uapress.arizona.edu

ISBN-13: 978-0-8165-4093-8 (paper)

Cover design by Leigh McDonald
Cover photo by S. N. Pattenden
Designed and typeset by Leigh McDonald in High Tower Text (display) and Times New
Roman 10.5/13

Excerpt from "Nearly Awake" from "Astrological Conundrums" from SELECTED
POEMS 1957-1994 by Ted Hughes. Copyright © 2002 by The Estate of Ted Hughes.
Reprinted by permission of Farrar, Straus and Giroux.

Publication of this book is made possible in part by the proceeds of a permanent endow-
ment created with the assistance of a Challenge Grant from the National Endowment for
the Humanities, a federal agency.

Library of Congress Cataloging-in-Publication Data
Names: Cahoon, Heather, (Heather M.), author.
Title: Horsefly dress : poems / Heather Cahoon.
Other titles: Sun tracks ; v. 87.
Description: Tucson : University of Arizona Press, 2020. | Series: Sun tracks: an American
    Indian literary series; 87
Identifiers: LCCN 2019046354 | ISBN 9780816540938 (paperback)
Subjects: LCSH: Salish Indians—Poetry. | LCGFT: Poetry.
Classification: LCC PS3603.A37858 A6 2020 | DDC 811/.6—dc23
LC record available at https://lccn.loc.gov/2019046354

Printed in the United States of America
♾ This paper meets the requirements of ANSI/NISO Z39.48-1992 (Permanence of Paper).

The cry you dare not cry in these moments
Will last you a lifetime.
—TED HUGHES, *WOLFWATCHING*

Contents

Horsefly Dress

Horsefly Dress

A long wing feather propels the stunted body
        of a black-crowned night heron through air,
   breaking apart
the dried mouth   of memory.

In an outpouring of   primordial story
   I hear her name: Čatnałqs

The hunting moon unearths Coyote's eldest and only daughter,
   her name no longer spoken   she turned
to porous stone.
   But I hear her name   Čatnałqs   along Flathead River
near Revais
         in the cutting of meat   its crackled
drying above smoldering cottonwood.

Čatnałqs   at the edge of river in passing water,
the embodiment of belief, she
         perforates the divide
   between known and unknown.   Here,
she reconsiders the archeology of our suffering.

Her mouth opens in the alarm cry of a brown thrasher,
a warning: *Brace for all that's wrapped into a name.*

Nunxʷé

Why this repeated sunburst
   of feathered
bodies

   cliff
swallow flocks
erupt

      into a sky

            of lungs

and throat

      a thousand
                        dull

brown wings

      frantically

                              folding

      releasing

      diffusing

light

      refracting

      reason

                              centrifugal

force(s)

d e c e n t r a l i z e

until

the   word

is

scrambled

un-   rec   og   ni z
able

uncomfortable

to look at
            as
                  this

history
                  of people (sqélixʷ) and place (šiyulexʷ)

                  so

difficult

to   under-

stand

            and   to

believe.

Remnant Nałisqélixʷ(tn)

Coyote steps out of an alder catkin, casts
his pelt aside and slips into a scene where
he can observe the monsters he didn't kill
before humans came to earth. He settles

on the outside of a glass viewing pane
behind which he sees a remnant nałisqélixʷ(tn),
its giant hands and mouth, keen nose pulling
the scent of sleeping children from the night.

The people-eating monster devours one child
and then another—wrist and belly, discarding
twists of tendon, the blaze of collarbone. Coyote
oozes his liver-red body through the pores

in the glass but he does not save the children.
No one does. Instead, he pulls from his head four
braids of sweet grass and smudges, filling the
room with smoke enough to cloud the memory.

Coyote and the Cross

I.

When the west surged into the center
of the world   the Word pulled back into heavy
honey-yellow lines
     and scarlet patches drawn
across the slight shoulders of certain blackbirds.

But reality rubs raw the wounds of all stories
     until the scoured bones of self-evidence
are all that's left.

Battling inside this orbed shell of space
we find   stories are no different
     from other living forms
the ragged-haired aligned
with every
primal instinct to avoid demise.

Consider Coyote, headbone raised to greet the night
song through black tree moss like witch's hair.
     He delivers a message
                    bound in the body
of unwritten texts. Like birds, ring-necked
     and refined, his cries confirm the un/believable.

II.

I count the breaths between bodies

    each syllable thrust from the chest—

      from Salish to English and back, Francis to Clara,

           Antoine/Atwén,   Malí Supí, through Supí,

    Pyél   back to X̱aliqs—or Shining Shirt,

the medicine person who saw men in long robes, the sign

    of a cross, saw it all

flung into being when,

    in slurred double whistles on the midwinter cusp

      of forest and field, a black-capped chickadee

sang the shadow sounds of his name.

    But even before that the forest stood smoldering,
    apparitions with arms raised toward the sky.

From Trees

each prayer
an open-
mouthed cry
sometimes   (silent)

hers
entered
this world
near
Box Elder
Creek
it hung
in the sky
above
her house
until
the week
following
Thanksgiving
when she
was found
in the
loose-leafed
air,
an ornament
swaying

Méstṁ /Lʔéw

In a farmer's field   open

as any   wound,   a robin's breast

flashes ocher red against the short-grazed

grass. It watches me in a way

that makes me wonder if it's my grandmother

the one   for whom

   my sister is named,

the one   who raised my father to be

all he is   and is not.

Your father lies buried   in the Jocko

        beneath birdsong

        the sorrow

   of snowmelt.   His body decayed

yet

   I feel   self-conscious revealing

his unbounded behavior.   Is it possible

he hears me,

possible

we own our stories

   in a way

that feels   like   trust?

You visit your father

   inside canyons where lodgepoles

stand in slanted half-light. You go there

to lift lichen

like scabs,   one for each instance

   of his tormenting affection,

complicated even in death.

The Origin of Death

Horsefly Dress carries her brother's baby
in her arms and remembers her father's stories
about how life on Earth began. She recalls
also the illness that took her from the world
of the living to a spirit world of waiting.
Upon her death, dazed heart like gravity pulling
him toward collapse, her father wandered. In his
grief he happened upon a river wide and rushing
happened to see his daughter on the other side.
Calling to her he demanded to cross over; he
could think of nothing else than seeing her again.
Although she refused at first, she took a canoe
to get him. As they cut cross current back
across the river she warned that he must not
interfere with the stick game being played.
He agreed but he did not keep his word. Instead,
he joined in the game, forever changing the nature
of life by inadvertently creating an opening for
the permanence of death. Horsefly Dress
chastised her father for ignoring her instructions,
for breaking his word, crying, *Now you have
killed me and your grandchildren forever. If
the other team had won we would have been
able to escape from this place of the dead.*

Horsefly Dress holds my brother's baby
in her arms amid the spirits on the other side.

Geography of Coyote

Coyote's lithe-limbed body grounds memory,
reconciles past with greater past. His dealings
are collected and recollected by people as far north
as Shuswaps down
    through dry Diné deserts
        and into Aztec arms. Coyote
is pivotal: a chokecherry seeded to generations
to aid survival.

We call him Snčĺép. He is married to Mole
and together they have several children—
    a daughter beautiful and kind
called Horsefly Dress   and four or five sons
depending on the story the teller the time
of year their names being
    He Knows as He Lays His Head Down,
        Lays Down Straight Under a Tree or Log,
    Excrement in the Middle Crook of His Foot
(alternatively sometimes called He Defecates on His Leg).
And then there is the fourth one,
Yelčńetpawastqn,
        a son a name unwilling
to be translated into English or to conform to any other
way of knowing. Last
but not least is He Washes His Feet, the baby.

Snčĺép is thick-haired and cunning,
    strategic, social, and selfish.
        Transformer of our world, redistributor
    of fire, food, and rights. Through a
complex pedagogy of contradiction, he demonstrates
    right ways of living.

To act like Snčlép is to behave foolishly.
To behave foolishly is to take action
against oneself; thus,
in Salish, a common root: nčípscut.

A Movement of Memory
in Two Parts

1.

Begin as you drive past Ninepipes,
past blue herons knee-deep
in marshy water, past the delicate tracks
left in shoreline mud by the air-boned
bodies of killdeers. Start there;
try remembering your most fleeting moments.
Reach back through the narrow fingers
of memory.

> I remember sitting with my siblings
> in the sunny backseat of a car. I remember
> looking at the seams in the tan vinyl seats.
> We were going to Charlo, driving
> past Ninepipes, on our way to visit
> our grandparents. Nothing about this trip
> stands out to make it unusual, yet
> the memory is there.

2.

Fallen snowberries sprinkle the dark ground
re-creating a night sky of found memories.
With eyes closed I move through them
intending to sever the blood-brittle ties
between us. I replay each memory slowly,
pausing inside rooms that hold so many

different depths of darkness. I am here,
an omniscient viewer. Quiet, I peer into corners
and closets, run my fingers over the pink
and red rose wallpaper, corners arching away
from the ceiling.

We are the series of moments we can remember.

Rescue

What becomes of the changes we attempt to will

into existence?   After a young friend's father dies

he stands before the bathroom mirror in darkness

and repeats,

Jesus, if you are real my father will be

next to me when I turn on the light.

But no matter how many times

the light flicks off and then on   his father never appears.

When I was a girl   some primal remnant sensed predation.

As still as stone in prayer for rescue

I closed my eyes

and

waited   waited   waited.   And I

escaped   but it was not the deliverance I had pled for.

My sister   in/discriminately sentenced

her small body

bared eyes eclipsed mouth lock-sealed around the stifled

cry that shakes me still   —and I,

I turned toward the wall and thought   *Better her than me.*

Łčíčše?

She is a wood warbler
hatched
    into madness.   She
emerged
from milky shell   earthen brown blotches
not Rorschach   not robin   but warbler.

Open-mouthed   swallow of hard-
chipped notes,   calls smothered
inside
    her smoke-gray chamber of throat.

Dis/appearing between branches
muted yellow-green
    tail feathers and body   dainty clawed toes
white lines half-circle   her eyes
sense but can't see
at the center of night   movements
misfire
misreads the body
          responds on its own.

A Recurring Dream

My sister two or three years old is taken by a man on a camel so out of place as he situates her on his lap then rides off atop the water. She is too young to mind the distance between us increasing as I—only six or seven myself—watch panicked from the rocky shoreline of our family's favorite campground on the west side of Flathead Lake. The man taking my sister is wearing a coat of many colors as I imagined Joseph's vertical stripes bright against the backdrop of dark mountains. I need to stop him to save her but I can't because even without trying I know I cannot walk on water.

Escape Routes

Each person has to create their own escape routes
from the situations they cannot tolerate.
—HELENA GOETHALS

My sister described to me how she raced her horse
bareback across the open plains of Kansas, described
the certainty of hooves connecting with dense earth, how she felt
the expanse and contraction of the horse's belly and the feeling
   of air,
which they burst into anew at every second, as the feeling
of complete   utter   presence,
the kind that insists you are powerful.

As a child I watched the wind reach
its fine fingers down the throat of my sister
and steal her breath so that her cries were silent.
As a child I understood that the past is a heavy burden
we carry like time.

My great-grandfather, my father, me, my sisters and brothers
each reached toward the unknown, a single breath split
between two spheres, one where it's okay to admit
we are powerless. This place
holds the many secrets of our past and we go there
in our dreams.

I awake inside a labyrinth of opposing geometric rooms and well-lit railed stairwells. I seek the source of a sound like fingernails grating in perfectly spaced intervals against a wall, the sound clear and loud in this odd space. I follow twisting stairways further and further up until I emerge into a room where four slanted glass ceilings meet just beyond my view. The sound almost unbearable as I approach and peer upward—a raven, feathers so black they emit blue highlights, hangs upside down like a bat, claws gripping tightly a sun-like glowing box at the highest apex of the ceiling, while a river otter struggles to unclasp its claws. Repeatedly the otter tries to force its long black fingernails beneath the raven's claws, making the awful sound, but the raven refuses to fall.

I awake a second time back in my own bed in the dark of night.

Unexceptional

A red fox knows her boundaries

in the foothill fields of the Missions.

This is unexceptional since it is common

among her kind. But sometimes irony

is quite harsh and the message she gets

is *You are unexceptional. Un-*

exceptional are you.

A Dream of Black Water

A sun-grayed dock wood swollen splintered by heat and rain stretches to the middle of an expanse of black water. At its end a wooden shack sits atop a meager floating deck where I stand watching my baby crawl toward me. I glance up to see two of my husband's friends walking out toward us when I hear my baby fall into the water glimpse him disappearing into the darkness—should I jump in after him I wonder panic-laced my body throat knowing I will be disoriented knowing I will lose this perspective from above where I can pinpoint the exact location I last saw him. I want my husband's friends to come and help I want to direct them to the place he disappeared but they are too far away. Indecision erodes as I recall that a baby submerged in water will always hold its breath. Peering into the dark water I make out my son's tiny body facing down slowly rising toward the surface. He is not frantic not thrashing not resisting caught in calmness he gradually ascends until he is within arm's reach. I pull him from the water and hold him to me as I stand up I look around; drought has killed everything as far as I can see on every side of the black lake stark golden desert unfolds its glistening sand formed by the wind into endless wavelike hills.

The Salish Root Word for Water

Half my life was lived in dreams of water. Night's long hours immersed me in standing, rushing, churning, falling, frozen water. *You are asking to be worthy of something*, says my friend. She tells me that the Salish root word for water is *séw,* a verb meaning to ask for permission or information, to make a plea to be worthy.

So much is said in this word: séwɬkʷ.

Peregrine Body

Hers   as mine is   a body
   in conflict

ever caught
between   flight and fight:

   I see her despite her silence
solitary   among the twisting

leaves
of chokecherries and ninebarks

her finely barred torso   flashes
into sight

   her slate gray scapulars   lift
open   twice she   fly-hops

among the brambles   then focuses
on me—

   mutual watchfulness reveals
that hers   as mine is   a body

in conflict   ever caught
   between   flight and fight.

Łx̣ʷłó Spq'ni?s

I.

The day is a memory
opened
   teeth to mouth in mourning

a cartogram of cornerings
   maps
the child's mind each
menacing impasse.

II.

A doe beds down
in the month of chokecherries a doe
beds down
   in the blonde hair   of a hill
alert
   even at rest   the felted brown
embodiment of vigilance.

        Hers   inborn
        ours
        a thing acquired.

III.

The irony of concealment is often
revelation
of one's true nature
        cutting lessons

these like violet thistles   thorns
    born   of woody taproots
stems webbed
with soft white hairs
spiraling my admission—

    In this month of chokecherries
    I cry   *I am sorry.*

Shelter

We wove hip-high field grass
into tunnels

knotting the tops
of bunched handfuls the drooping
heads tied together.

My seven siblings and I
sheltered ourselves

inside these labyrinths
in a galaxy of grasses.

Perilous

By nature, we know a thing through its absence.
Within this world of interlocked dichotomies the sliding scale
is king.   A case in point:

A northern pygmy owl, barely sparrow-sized, flew into our large
window reflecting sky and mountains and fell unconscious
to the weathered floorboards of our deck.

My brother Brian carried it inside cradled in the temporary
casket of his hands. Eventually, its eyes blinked open—but
despite potential peril, its heartbeat was not raucous,
it made no escape attempts.

For hours, it sat with wings neatly folded at its sides, plumped
white chest relaxed, content to watch my family go about
their day. Even when brought back outside
it lingered, loath to leave
my brother's open palm.

Its reaction, so different from another I spotted in bare late fall
branches a few feet from a trail. This diurnal hunter only let me
get so close
before leaping into heavy flight.

                        When bravery loses ground,
it slides toward fear
then falls to flight inside the mind of a northern pygmy owl
    hidden behind large lemon yellow eyes.

A Child's Funeral

I find myself in the building where I attended church as a child. I sit fingering my wrists, feeling for my bison horn bracelets, gifts from my father that I wear for good luck. But who needs luck at a funeral I think, mind wander to a study that found unanswered prayers are the primary reason people abandon faith in their god. I consider this idea of reciprocal abandonment, slip questions of the forsaken back to when I was a girl back further still to a most famous cry of the damned, *Eli, Eli, lema sabachthani?*

Meditations on Blue

open as sky as belief   my son's eyes as a child
before they shifted to earth-grounded hues of tufted hairgrass golden
star moss and devil's club leaves

six mountain bluebirds frozen in space but not time with the help
of the wild wind   against the blonde hillside they appear as if
in a still life as if I could walk up and pluck one from midair

fireflies like blue-white micro stars blink
on-off near my father's house on Post Creek   quickly
they disappear into the dark mouth of night

an emotion described as in "s/he is feeling blue"
an idiom incapable of posing the questions cried by those it depicts
if crisis truly carries opportunity what of the recursive nature
of loss   where is the exit from ruin

because qʷáy the word for blue also describes my concepts
of black and green   I attempt to reconcile these differing
perspectives held captive in a word

in keen self-awareness of other she (i.e., meaning) is
the reckoning found inside ir*recon-*
cilable   or the irreconcilable inside found reckoning   whichever

it is   she (i.e., meaning) sometimes enters the mind
from the outside over-   stepping the insoluble the wood planked
borders between meanings   as if

one word or idea was (or is)
more or less active in the mouth the mind   or in protest
or pronoun   as if

any idea can fit inside the carcass-like
casket of label

I read that *we categorize to create meaning therefore it is possible to change meaning by recategorizing*

meaning hovers a hummingbird moth—or is it
the real thing   which again is it (Trochilidae or łxʷxʷni) the buzzing
long-beaked seeker of nectar that never seems to alight

Čatnałqs

Swirling inside *ch*   into *cha-*   *tin-*   *alks*

   a wild crocus, shoots reaching down into their proper place

unchanged for twelve thousand years—all because

      her father agreed to rid the world of nałisqélixʷ(tn)

the people-eating monsters the short-faced the grizzled ice

everywhere the saber-toothed chill

of a world

slowly thawing.

Rilke, Screech Owl, and Night Loons

1.

If *all art is the result*
of one's having been in danger
what is created when a girl walks
beaten and burned for four miles
before collapsing
into stillness.

-

Across the shadow-blue river
from hunting camp near Perma
a screech owl brings nightfall
as she alights on a nearby
lightning-struck snag burnt ash
black from inside out. She trains
her blazoned eyes on me
and calls through darkness.

We stare at each other as she calls
and calls then departs into the night.
Follow me she seems to urge
and for a moment I almost do—
but I know this omen of endings.

Shortly she returns, closer this time,
and calls out again and again and I
wonder what death will strike.

2.

A screech owl brings a curious death
under a mother-of-pearl moon and I begin
to see the disembodied in gas stations
and convenience stores, human
carcasses all, hollowed by unearned
battering or priggish arrogance.

Within this violent tug-of-war
of mortality circumstance preys on
so many, bleeds holes in the assertion
of any ultimate equalizing factor.
Head and eyes drawn down begins
the pattern followed by curl of body,
cervical to sacral, until each one
has reassumed their first
their fetal   shape.

-

Horsefly Dress tries to believe
there are no casualties. She lifts
her head and scans the October night
air, wet dark blue, for something
that cuts the white noise of living.

A pair of loons calls out from the
dark heavens
punctured   by pinholes of light.

Ode to Pulia, Every Mother

A mother myself   I find her in pieces

  of every tight piercing cry of alarm

the sharp-shinned hawk   precursor

to regret   for one or more

  many times over.   But I wish to unravel

this inherent confusion this umbilical expectation

  cordage of dogbane and birthright strung

between offspring and mother

twined into the act   of birth giving,

  that seemingly

immortalizing ritual

wherein

the first mother

is each one thereafter   passing

her blood and being on   and on

and on.

Thus, we sometimes hold our

im/mortal mothers   as arnica, the fragrance of yarrow,

each one the larkspur and lupines of summer

venerations these

lofty projections

expectations to be softness the safety of nest before feathers

or teeth.

But none of this   will ever do

　　because how we   experience m/other

frames the first iteration of self

frames all

that follows.

Death as a Lens

Expose: To make bare, to uncover, to disclose.
A male ruffed grouse lies lifeless, neck
limp, eyelids soft. He would be food
and so much more. Crouching so my sons
could see, my father slit open the delicate
casing of his craw, exposing whole snowberries
in perfect whiteness, crisp and toothy
emerald ninebark leaves nestling tiny
brown seeds and buffalo berries
still crimson red.   Seeing
the innermost contents of his body revealed
his recent unobserved behavior and brought
two separate moments of intimate exposure
into curious alignment:

Nefariousness   forced itself
when I was a child   witness
to human cruelty
and whole detachment   I had not known
existed. Brutality   bore down,
*   direct and blatant,*
so unabashed in its delivery—
the sharpest knowing is with one's eyes.

A Dream of Black Crows

My brother Daniel and another friend and I stand at the edge of a creek runoff wide and wild they walk into the water and are swept out of sight. With meadowlark heart beating I wade in after them the current steals my footing sucking me beneath the surface where the water is unmoving clear and silent the creek bed a road of richly colored stones haloed in streaks of sunlight. The urge to breathe brings me to the surface. I raise my head above water to find I am racing backward downstream engulfed in the full fury of raging current. Atop the steep embankment to my right old growth ponderosas stand in perfect uniformity thick reddish-brown bark deeply fault lined needles spiking green into the pewter sky. Above them one hundred black crows fly upstream. They are pregnant and their eggs fall from them in flight. I hear the eggs shatter against the earth but I also hear the piercing cries of fledglings.

ScX'lil

1.

Arrow-leaved balsamroot bones
cover the hillside. Their dried foliage
rustles, brittle leaves rub one on another
mimicking a rattlesnake warning
that shakes me back to the trail
and my four-year-old son hiking in front.
I hear him say, "Mom, pretend we are lions,"
then I pause as he repeats what I whisper
to him each night as he shifts into sleep:
We are brave and we are safe.

2.

How to describe energy without matter,
without dimension or gods. A holiness
filled the hospital room the moment
of his birth. He was born still and then
held in tight familial embrace. We felt
the slight weight of his body, the largeness
of his being, an incorporeal force
filling the room like light, or scent,
uncontainable, a pervasive medium
that all-encompassed us in knowing.

3.

The most difficult death is forgiveness,
a basket woven from reeds of resentment
and sorrow reworked into useful form.

It is the act of re-striking the delicate
balance between grievance and absolution
from perceived wrong actions or events,
those ephemeral instances that impart
lasting effects. May I realize this most
difficult death as a catalyst for life.

Render

May I be worthy

of my most embattled moments.

May I find a way   to render meaning

from the blood-marbled memories

cached inside

the carcass of the past.

To Forge Meaning

for dg

I.

This day is edged like a coarsely toothed leaf.

I am back on my reservation, home, at least for the moment.

Driving above Dixon, I wonder as I watch a grouse hen lead

her babies across an old logging road if I will ever

not be pulled home, ever not feel myself lingering

    between the past   and present   places

I call home.

II.

None of us has been immune from our shared history

   of push

and push

back,   the momentum of which

has propelled us

to the present moment.

III.

This moment has been made   by meteors

      cutting through darkness

           in the densely starred sky

above Blue Bay, the birth

      of my two sons, the death

of certain fears and the

           forging of meaning

from what remains.

IV.

Meaning is pulled like feathers from tightly wound days, it is

made from the least and most of the mundane,   from what

wills itself into existence—   whatever inks itself

onto the page.

A Dream of Wolves

Standing in an open field near Charlo a gray wolf stares my way, another wolf stands next to him with his back to me. The second wolf runs backward toward me as if in a movie played in reverse. Frightened I try not to run begin quickly stepping away but it is not enough. When he is just ten feet from me he turns and peers at me his eyes portals to the other world. Without warning he charges toward me then impact: we scuffle in a terror-filled blur of movements until I awake to find myself in a blurred battle with what I see is a wolf as he exits the fight and backs quickly away. When he is ten feet from me he pauses stares at me behind his piercing gaze the other world opens. With mounting conviction I step toward him quickly to scare him away. Frightened he turns from me and flees to the safety of another wolf that is standing in an open field near Charlo.

X̣ʷell

Left again

an infant air-sucks

itself into malnourished

sleep.

With no teeth

in sight for months

he dreams he is

Ćaẇcínšn,

Coyote's baby and favorite son,

carried

on his father's

back.

A Dream of a Darling Boy

Is this boy my father? I wondered later upon waking. He was a boy from home that much I could recognize his dark hair lively eyes glossy black a muted smile I could only describe as darling. I am walking with my sister near Dixon, Flathead River to the north, the snow deep maybe four feet. We visit as we walk on an elevated wooden structure a sidewalk of sorts paralleling the highway. Mid-sentence I sense someone behind us, looking back I see this boy. He appears to be three or four years old he is bashful he is shirtless shoeless has no jacket, clothed only in a pastel yellow shortsuit, a romper, thin straps stemming from waistband up over bare shoulders back down to opposite waistband in back. Why is he all alone? It is winter why is he not properly dressed? And why does he not seem to mind the cold? I wonder as I glance down at his feet frostbitten freezer-burned flesh dry and cracking each toe the whole foot and ankles eating its way up his small legs. He smiles at me but keeps a safe distance this little boy who earlier I described as darling who, on second thought, is more accurately described as daring, kʷtispúʔu: he dares to be.

Sharp

A micro moth
flutter-bumps
against the moon
triggering

the movement
of a nighthawk
into flight,
tempering the rite
of passage
through birth canal
into being
for every child
left to chance.

This world
of the living
is rationed, is
a sharp-
shinned hawk
who, without
malice or remorse
feeds her babies
the nestlings
she finds
in other nests.

WASP

A conversation exists beyond reach.
You hear it beneath the sound
of paper-crisp wings, see colonies
busy building their homes on your land.
With self-privileged aggression
they silence your protests, force open
your mouth, reach in until they hold
in their hand the part of your body
that houses your voice, twisting
and pulling it from you. But
because you have drawn strength
from this landscape for millennia,
you survive. Coyote and Spider,
Muskrat and Raven refuse
to allow their transformative work
in this place to have been in vain.
Coyote trots near your feet, keeps Fox
at his side and together they keep you alive,
moving systematically from person to person
instigating rebirths and exactly the right
challenges you need to overcome
every weakness you have. *Learn this*
foreign language, they heed. This language
of laws, of perceived rights that privilege
only one small way of being. *Know this*,
they whisper into your dreams:
The day before the first foreigner
set foot on this land, this entire story
played out in the sky. Some
of your old people saw it. Hear their songs
beneath the white noise made

by the paper-winged wasps. Have faith
that these songs will come through to clarity.
Open your mouths and let out your breath,
let it form the ideas whose first step toward
realization is articulation. Believe
that the paper-winged buzz will weaken
and become ever fainter until
the only sound left is that of your singing.

Red Osier Spiders

The color of cut flesh, red osier
dogwood spires sever
the white snow alongside
the narrow canal roads crawling
through Jocko Canyon. These
canals were built by suyuyapi
one hundred years ago to advance
only the interests of yeomen farmers,
foreigners who imported inside
seed bags and bibles another
framework for viewing all things.

The second past dusk my smallest
son sees what I cannot—the giant spiny
spiders with no eyes or face skittering
across the airspace in my bedroom.

Unéx^w

Which is the real world

    when language is scaffold for knowing

when   can one ever trust what they see

with the eye-less words

    they've been given?   Words

invert

cling   to ceilings

hang

like bats drop

    mouthfuls of words

I cannot open.

Unseen archers fire   words like rosewood arrows

that pierce the airy sky of flesh

    in a confrontation between past and present knowing

that spills   injured

          and dying

words

across valleys and pages of memory.

The Hawk Who Wears an Owl's Face

Chance turns my eyes   to her perch

    where she flashes between beings

or bodies. She splits in two as she lifts into flight

I see   she is a northern harrier

the hawk

who wears an owl's face.

The owl   I thought she was remains

bark-bound dissipates

    slowly subsumed by the warm wing

        song murmurs

of bald-faced hornets,

their large kidney-shaped eyes

onyx and glossy.

Baby Out of Cut-Open Woman

so-called because he was sckʷełʼelénč, "cut out of the stomach"
as an infant.   Indeed, he survived the un/believable, a lucky
    break,
to become the only living member of his immediate family.

Another lucky break, he won his race against the cold birds,
earning the right
to make a law that they could no longer control
all the weather,
ending the age of ice.

Next, he gathered his families' bones
their marrowed limbs, each rib, forearm,
and finger.
                Covering them with his blanket, he jumped over
                            four times,
bringing them,
each one
back
to life.

-

These are the stories that belong here,
that pushed up through this soil unfurling
as arrow-leaved balsamroot leaves and boulders found in
    unusual
places.

How else does a thing enter this world
now so changed we struggle to hear the shapes of a language
    that no longer fits every ear?
Each story word frag-
                    ment   moves
over hills the highest reaches of trees
    without catching in memory.   But

the crispness of Snlaq̓éy of Kʷĺncutn like fire
crackle the flick of sound a body remembers.

Meta

Transformation always and in everything as in even

false hellebore

recognizes the convertibility

of all phenomena, the recasting of one thing

into another,

> as in Spokani became the sun as in Coyote is a man
> is an animal is a teacher repeatedly killed and reborn.

> He suffers an endless series of deaths, some metaphorical some
> metaphysical, each one metamorphic.

A Dream of Shifting Faces

Two women enter the darkened room speaking in hushed voices they sit at the foot of the bed next to mine. Still trapped in middle consciousness I try to see if they are really there but it is so dark I cannot tell if my eyes are closed or open. Suddenly I see my grandmother who died years earlier and with whom I was so close. We embrace and I am filled equally with grief and gratitude. She is so familiar her face of love and kindness but why her aged appearance—why in spirit does she look as she had in death? All at once upon this wondering her blue irises bleed to deepest brown soft gray curls lengthen to sleek black as her skin smooths backward into youth, the face of a stranger.

Magpies

A magpie flock float-jumps down the hill from one tree
to another bypassing us on the short switchbacks
a game of leapfrog   a winged cacophony of chatter and black-
    blue iridescent bodies their tails flight feathers fanned
white wingtips flashing.

After three passes   they cut quickly to the bottom clustering
in a stunted serviceberry bush tangle of offshoots near its base
hardly large enough to hold them all.
My young son dashes
    toward them not to capture or frighten but for glee
that of a child
the fun and freedom found in racing toward a treasure.

Nevertheless   they disperse an ellipsis shattered black-bodied
bird dots scatter in all directions   their absence revealing
    a gift tucked snugly amongst branches
its blue packaging unmistakable unopened—   tobacco.
We use it to make an offering   an earnest prayer of thanks:

Earlier near the hilltop among so many trailside forget-me-nots
    diminutive bright sky-blue petals with white starred
centers   goldenrod iris and storm-cloud pupils eyes
nonetheless   watching witness to the omen
of the pygmy owl manifesting as the death of pernicious
preoccupation and remnant terror
the slow release
    of bluebirds
trapped inside
my throat.

Orb Weavers

Sunlight shifts snow from solid
   to liquid form and gravity takes it to lower ground.
            It pauses to pool in Upper and Lower Terrace Lakes
            then merges into a stream that feeds Swartz, another
            micro body of low mountain water, before exiting
            the foothills in fast streams bordered by stones
            draped in bottle moss.

The olive-lime green moss leaves curve
   and gradually narrow to a point beneath petite urn-shaped
            capsules that seal in the soft silence of their moist
            montane home. I was there with my family one
            summer when I was nothing but boiling blood
            and body, struggling to align the loose star shoots
            of my teenage mind.

Approaching the trailhead
   I saw the nesting ground of spiders, five or six
            plump bellied orb weavers clutching unseen webs
            just off the ground. True to adaptation's intent,
            they drew me in close enough to touch, near enough
            to see that they were merely feigning
            their arachnid form.

These mountain lady's slipper
   orchids imitating orb weavers, hung belly-up,
            their twisting sepal tendrils forming legs, long
            and brown, arching away from either bulging bellies
            or ellipsoid labellum capsules, both white with
            mauve speckles and striation, both filled with seed
            for future young.

Rebirth and the Almost Moon

Trace it back, movement along jagged horizon, to the time Coyote and Antelope sent their sons to steal the night sun. But the moon was the favorite plaything of a certain tribe of animal people and they were not about to let it go without a fight. However, Coyote's sons were cunning, capturing the moon. Outsmarted owners in close pursuit they raced through forest across plain until Coyote's sons began to tire; thus, stretch of ankle met mouth, trip to fatal fall of teeth and bone. As heartbeats slowed they tossed the moon to the Antelope brothers and the chase continued. Antelope's sons ran like lightning and made it home. Upon presenting their father and Snčíép with the moon prize and the story of Coyote's sons' deaths, Coyote bent hollow-mouthed howl crying as only a father can. He took the moon back to its owners to make a deal: he would return the moon if they would return his sons to life. They agreed and one by one, Coyote's sons' hearts resumed beating, chests rise-falling, wrists pulsing, until their amber eyes blinked on like stars.

Acknowledgments

I am fortunate to have many people to thank. First, my family, all lineages and generations but especially my parents, my father, Francis Cahoon (and his amazing wife, Carol), for his fierce loyalty and bravery, and my mother, Nancy Niemeyer Eastham (and her husband, Jim), for her quiet strength and unshakable love. My siblings—Christy, Francis, Jody, Eldon, Daniel, Brian, Kelsey, and Jamie—whose perseverance, goodness, and companionship throughout childhood and adulthood provides the fodder for so many of these poems, as do the places and stories that we inhabit together. My husband, Jesse King, our sons, Reynolds and Eres. My extended family including my grandmother, Thelma Dixon Niemeyer; and all my aunties, uncles, and cousins; and my in-laws, particularly Marti de Alva and lifelong friend Genevieve Elena King, as well as Faith Price, Angelina Urbina, and Vanina Herrera.

Lémlmtš to Johnny and the late Joan Arlee, and to Tony Incashola, for always being willing to share their knowledge and for their tireless work to preserve Séliš and Qĺispé culture and language. My gratitude also goes to Vance Home Gun for reviewing the glossary of Salish words that appears at the end of this collection; many of these definitions were adapted from *Seliš Nyoʔnuntn: Medicine for the Salish Language, 2nd edition*, by Tachini Pete. Thanks also to my craft and creative mentors, especially dg nanouk okpik, Sandra Alcosser, and the late Patricia Goedicke, as well as to Heather E. Bruce, Sherwin Bitsui, Kate Shanley, David Moore, Robert Stubblefield, Gabriella Gutierrez y Muhs, and Natalie Peeterse of Open Country Press, for lending their support and for providing insightful comments and editing suggestions.

I also gratefully acknowledge the Montana Arts Council for their 2015 Artist Innovation Award, which enabled me to begin this collection of poems. And finally, my thanks to the editors of the following publications, where versions of these poems have appeared:

Academy of American Poets Poem-a-Day, "Lčíčše?"

American Indian Culture and Research Journal, "Peregrine Body" (published as "Peregrine"), "Shelter," and "Ode to Pulia"

basalt, "Remnant Nałisqélixʷ(tn)," "Čatnałqs," "Dream Series in Three Parts" ("A Dream of Crows," "A Dream of Wolves," "A Dream of a Darling Boy"), "Baby Out of Cut-Open Woman"

basalt online, "Coyote and the Cross" and "Meta"

Bright Bones: Contemporary Montana Writing, "Escape Routes" and "Magpies" (published as "Revision")

Burnside Review, "Sharp"

Camas: The Nature of the West, "Horsefly Dress"

Carve Magazine, "Death as a Lens"

Cutthroat: A Journal of the Arts, "WASP"

Hanging Loose, "A Recurring Dream" and "The Salish Root Word for Water"

LitHub, "Nunxʷé" and "Rebirth and the Almost Moon"

Poems Across the Big Sky II: An Anthology of Montana Poets, "Méstm̓/ Lʔéw" and "Geography of Coyote"

Poetry Northwest, "Ł̣xʷłó Spq'niʔs" and "Rescue"

South Dakota Review, "The Origin of Death," "Perilous," and "Orb Weavers"

Southern Humanities Review online, "Red Osier Spiders"

Verde Que Te Quiero: Poems after Federico Garcia Lorca, "Red Osier Spiders"

Yellow Medicine Review, "Meditations on Blue," "To Forge Meaning" and "Unéxʷ"

Glossary of Salish Words

AMOTQN. Creator, literally "He Who Sits on Top"; president. From *emut* (root meaning to sit) and *qin, qn* (suffix meaning top)

ATWÉN. Antoine, a man's name

ČATNAŁQS. Horsefly Dress (Coyote and Mole's only daughter). From *čatnałq* (horsefly) and *ištpálqs* (dress/skirt—from *lqs, alqs*, suffix meaning clothes)

KʷĹNCUTN. Creator, Maker of Ways/Mannerisms, also referred to as Amotqn or Great Spirit. From *cut* (root meaning one's mannerisms), *kʷĺ* (prefix meaning to make), and *tin, tn* (suffix meaning by means of/device)

KʷTISPÚʔU. Brave; literally "big heart"

ŁČÍČŠEʔ. Older sister

ŁX̣ʷŁÓ SPQ'NIʔS. Month of the chokecherries, the Salish name for the month of September

ŁX̣ʷX̣ʷNI. Hummingbird

MALÍ SUPÍ. Mary Sophie, a woman's name

MÉSTṀ/LʔÉW. Her father (girl's father) / His father (boy's father)

NAŁISQÉLIXʷ(TN). People-eating monsters that roamed the earth terrorizing and devouring humans until Coyote killed them, making the earth suitable for human habitation. From *nałisqé* (monster) and *sqélixʷ* (human, person, American Indian; literally, "flesh/meat of the earth"—from *sqeltč* [meat] and *sťulixʷ* [land or earth])

NČĹPSCUT. To act like Coyote, to be foolish, to mimic others' actions just because they are doing it. From Snčĺep (root meaning Coyote) and *cut* (suffix meaning action to the self)

NUNXʷÉ. Believe

PULIA. Mole, Coyote's wife, alternatively spelled Puɫyahá

PYÉL. Peter, a man's name

QʷÁY. Blue. On the spectrum of color this word describes the lighter tones of blue while the darker tones would be described with the word for black. The word used to describe green also includes some of the blue spectrum. This is the reason why the word for blue sky uses the descriptor green and the word for watermelon uses the descriptor blue.

SCKʷEŁT'ELÉNČ. "Cut out of the stomach," the name of the part of the weather, or a weather being, whose actions brought about the end of the last Ice Age

SCƛ'LIL. Death

SÉWŁKʷ. Water. From *séw* (action root word indicating inquiring for information or permission) and *łkʷ* (suffix indicating liquid)

ŠIYULEXʷ. First land, homeland, place of origin

SNČ̓ĹÉP. Coyote

SNLAQ̓ÉY. Sweat lodge

SPOKANI. Son of Amotqn, the Creator

SQÉLIXʷ. Human, person, American Indian; literally, "flesh/meat of the earth"—from *sqeltč* (meat) and *sťulixʷ* (land or earth)

SUPÍ. Sophie, a woman's name

SUYUYAPI. The plural of *suyapi* (white person), meaning white people, or people of Euro-American descent

UNÉXʷ. Real, true, yes

X̣ALL̓QS. Shining Shirt, a Séliš-Ql̓ispé visionary

X̣ʷELL. S/He was abandoned, thrown away, left behind

YELČN̓ETPAWASTQN. Coyote and Mole's fourth son

Notes

This collection of poems takes as its title the name of Coyote and Mole's only daughter, Čatnałqs, or Horsefly Dress. It also alludes to a handful of Séliš and Qĺispé stories that have been told since time immemorial. Some of these are Coyote stories, or sqʷllumt, sacred stories chronicling the creation and transformation of the world. Because they explain the nature of our existence and of the Creator, Amotqn, they are analogous to the revealed scriptures of other spiritual traditions. As a result, tribal protocol relegates sharing them in their entirety or discussing them at length to the winter months when snow is on the ground. Although they appear in this book, these stories belong to the entire tribal community, past, present, and future. Additionally, not all of the references to Coyote, Mole, and Horsefly Dress come from traditional stories; sometimes they have been pulled into contemporary contexts and personal situations where their relevance to daily life remains unchanged.

Page 17. The situation referenced and the lines quoted in italics in the first stanza, "Jesus, if you are real my father will be / next to me when I turn on the light," come from Kevin Kicking Woman's play, *The Sun as My Witness.*

Page 31. The italicized words, *Eli, Eli, lema sabachthani,* are reported in Matthew 27:46 as being the final words cried by Jesus. They translate into English as "My God, my God, why have you forsaken me?"

Page 38. The italicized quote, "we categorize to create meaning therefore / it is possible / to change meaning by recategorizing," is taken from Lisa Feldman Barrett's book, *How Emotions Are Made: The Secret Life of the Brain* (Houghton Mifflin Harcourt, 2017).

Page 41. The opening partial quote in italics, "all art is the result / of one's having been in danger," as well as several color references throughout the poem, are taken from Rainer Maria Rilke's book, *Letters on Cézanne* (Fromm International Publishing Corporation, 1985).

Page 47. In the second stanza, the italicized lines, "How to describe energy without matter, / without dimension or gods," are excerpted from Mei-Mei Berssenbrugge's poem, "Immortals Having a Party" in her book, *Hello, the Roses* (New Directions, 2013).

About the Author

HEATHER CAHOON, PhD, is an award-winning poet and a scholar of federal Indian policy. She is from the Flathead Reservation in western Montana, where she is a member of the Confederated Salish and Kootenai Tribes.